30 Minutes
...To Improve Your
Telesales Techniques

D0589102

30 Minutes
...To Improve Your
Telesales Techniques

Chris De Winter

KOGAN PAGE

First published in the UK by Kogan Page, 2000

Apart from any fair dealing for the purposes of research or private study, or criticism or review, as permitted under the Copyright, Designs and Patents Act 1988, this publication may only be reproduced, stored or transmitted, in any form or by any means, with the prior permission in writing of the publishers, or in the case of reprographic reproduction, in accordance with the terms and licences issued by the Copyright Licensing Agency. Enquiries concerning reproduction outside those terms should be sent to the publishers at the undermentioned address:

Kogan Page Limited
120 Pentonville Road
London N1 9JN

© Chris De Winter, 2000

The right of Chris De Winter to be identified as author of this work has been asserted by her in accordance with the Copyright, Designs and Patents Act 1988.

British Library Cataloguing in Publication Data
A CIP record for this book is available from the British Library.

ISBN 0 7494 3190 3

Typeset by Florence Production Ltd, Stoodleigh, Devon

Printed and bound in Great Britain by Clays Ltd, St Ives plc

CONTENTS

The 30 Minutes Series

The *Kogan Page 30 Minutes Series* has been devised to give your confidence a boost when faced with tackling a new skill or challenge for the first time.

So the next time you're thrown in at the deep end and want to bring your skills up to scratch or pep up your career prospects, turn to the *30 Minutes Series* for help!

Titles available are:

30 Minutes Before a Meeting

30 Minutes Before a Presentation

30 Minutes Before Your Job Interview

30 Minutes To Boost Your Communication Skills

30 Minutes To Brainstorm Great Ideas

30 Minutes To Deal with Difficult People

30 Minutes To Make the Right Decision

30 Minutes To Make the Right Impression

30 Minutes To Master the Internet

30 Minutes To Plan a Project

30 Minutes To Prepare a Job Application

30 Minutes To Succeed in Business Writing

30 Minutes To Write a Business Plan

30 Minutes To Write a Marketing Plan

30 Minutes To Write a Report

30 Minutes To Write Sales Letters

Available from all good booksellers.
For further information on the series, please contact:

Kogan Page, 120 Pentonville Road, London N1 9JN
Tel: 020 7278 0433 Fax: 020 7837 6348

INTRODUCTION

So you want a crash course in improving your telesales technique? Selling over the phone is a skill involving people. Those people are our customers and if we don't take care of them someone else will. In today's increasingly competitive business world the correct management of our customers is becoming an even more demanding task. In addition to keeping our existing customers happy and to maintain a competitive edge, we must also expand our client base. That means bringing new business on board and potentially involving many more members of the company in increasing business. Indeed, 80 per cent of all business is conducted over the telephone.

Unfortunately, while recognizing the enormous contribution the phone makes in business, companies have been known to employ staff, sit them at a desk with a phone and expect immediate results, without properly equipping them for the job. Similarly, many of the professional bodies that have previously relied on the 'old boy network' to bring in business are now finding themselves in a situation where they must become proactive. This means picking up the phone themselves and contacting prospects. Many feel anxious and unable to communicate effectively in this way. Anxieties can prompt a bad impression, leading to poor results, which will cause further damage by creating a despondent you! Point taken?

How you view the phone is the very key to its success. We live in a world where records and achievements are constantly changing. Just look at the Internet – the speed at which it opens doors is phenomenal. Yet, although technology is providing a number of different means through which business can be conducted it is sometimes easy to lose sight of the fact that business is transacted between people – people with needs and expectations and people who can help meet these needs.

Because of the demands on us we often tackle things with haste, quickly adding to something that may actually not be accurate or appropriate. Indeed, all too often we compound the problem. For that reason this book aims to tackle the issues at source – in other words to help you look at your abilities from scratch. Whatever your level of expertise you need to take stock and, to make sure you don't develop any bad habits, to go back to the beginning and build anew. We can't afford to stay still. We have to sharpen our skills and broaden our horizons to stay competitive.

1

BACK TO BASICS

People who have been in sales for a number of years will appreciate that part of the fun in the job is that you are always learning. You can never be in a position to say 'I know it all' because the world we live in is constantly changing.

Impressions

Anyone dealing with customers is giving vital impressions. The reputation of the whole company depends on your attitude. You have your finger on the pulse of your customers. You can examine their needs, their buying trends, likes and dislikes, how they perceive you and so on. While this can be hugely rewarding, like anything it needs to be worked at. The stakes are high. You never get a second chance to make a good impression or indeed maintain a good impression.

To tackle the task of improving your skills you need to go back to basics – wipe the slate clean and start from scratch. Whatever your ability in telesales or your level of expertise in your profession, to successfully review you need to try to keep an open mind. As we approach each area you can then build in your own material as an enhancing tool. If you try to do it the other way around, ie slot new information into your existing technique, you may find that you are building on the present problems you have developed. Ultimately you will have a new and fresh approach to compare with your existing technique and then you may judge for yourself how best to move forward.

Angle

On a chat show recently, guidance was given to new comedians by experienced performers. Quite simply it was to imagine that you were playing a game that had certain rules. You learn them, acquire the skills and techniques to command the game and adapt your style to suit. They stressed the importance of 'being yourself' and not trying to be the next Victoria Wood or whoever, but rather the next you! This suits our purpose too. You see it helps to dispel any myth that 'telephone cloning' is required. Successful communicators do not lose their own identity. The customer is the purchaser and our job is to satisfy the customer's needs, which also fulfils a goal within our company. The customer will relate to you first, and without identity this is impossible. We need to remain individual while demonstrating elements of the negotiator. Naturally we will aim to satisfy our own targets and goals by persuading a customer or prospect to buy our products or service, but we are *not* con merchants with the 'gift of he gab' and our customers' needs must also be met. Striking a balance between the two parties is essential. But how?

Communication

In good communication we need to strike a balance between talking and listening to make it two way. In order to put a customer's mind at rest so that he or she will start listening we have to demonstrate that we can be trusted.

The wrong approach

Your approach is of paramount importance to the success of each call. To demonstrate this, try this simple exercise. You will need the assistance of another person. Ask them to hold up their right hand, palm facing towards you. You hold up your left hand, then by mirroring make contact by touching palms. Suggest that you both apply pressure to each other and see what happens. Usually, whether you push lightly or firmly, so does your partner. The result is the hands remain in the same position. Each person absorbs the impact of the pressure the partner applies and then responds with an equal amount of pressure. It would be rare indeed if anyone doing this exercise allows their hand to be pushed away completely.

So what's happening? Each person is resisting the other's push. They are absorbing the other's pressure. Without prior warning you will have demonstrated that people resist pushiness or being pushed. If you now apply this idea to approaching your customers you will see that diplomacy is going to be vitally important. Nobody responds well to being forced.

The right approach

Although customers do not like being pushed or coerced, they will be led or guided. Think about the working sheep-dog. How does he lead the sheep into the pen? To watch and admire this art is fascinating. The dog almost guides from an unobtrusive position, making his presence known from the back, allowing the sheep to focus on and then move towards the pen. Rather than manipulate he has helped manoeuvre them in such a way that the decision the sheep make is the one the dog intended but there has been no force applied.

Your customers will want to make a good decision when they buy something. They don't want to be forced or told or sold to. It's far better to allow customers the opportunity to convince themselves.

Additional factors

The key to success is good communication skills and the vision to look broadly at the task in hand. Take driving as an analogy. It isn't enough to be able to drive your own car: you must consider all the others on the road, antici-pate their movements and be aware of all the other factors – pedestrians, road signs, weather conditions and so on. In sales, no two calls are the same because of who is on the other end of the line, and the differing products and services sold. People involved in telesales are faced with constant challenges.

Psychology

Selling over the phone is a skill. It is a skill in which psychology is a key feature. The differences between a successful call and an unsuccessful one can be marginal, but enough to make a difference. This is why cloning was mentioned. It is so important to free yourself of any old habits and approach this now with a clean slate. Try to pick up information as if for the first time by eliminating any preconceptions you may have. All too often in their eagerness to use the correct techniques, people can sound 'brain washed' and unnatural.

As our potential clients cannot see us, they will judge our expertise and professionalism as we project them over the phone. However, our competitors are equally equipped, so why should our clients buy from us? While applying techniques and maintaining a smooth approach you must also preserve your own personality. In other words, you will adapt the rules of the game by allowing customers to warm to your individualism. The quickest route to success is to appear to be playing by other people's rules when in fact you are playing by your own. Think for a moment of yourself window-shopping. A sales assistant approaches you, you talk and then you return home happy and tell your family that you have bought a special present for a friend whose birthday is next month. You were not looking for a birthday present on this occasion and yet you bought. You don't say that the shop assistant *sold* the item to you – if you did, you would have been acutely aware of sales pressure. You *bought* it. This is one of the keys to successful selling – remember, nobody likes to admit to being sold anything but they can be persuaded to buy. Our customers and prospects will buy provided you understand their needs, know how to persuade them and indeed how to develop that awareness of need within the customer (remember the sheep?).

Dispel your fears

We all know the saying, 'A bad workman blames his tools'. The phone is no exception. It is astonishing that in business today there are still such strong feelings surrounding the use of the telephone as a sales tool. Comments such as, 'It's so transparent', 'I wouldn't give anyone the time/ take the call', 'People prefer face-to-face contact', 'It's just a con', and so on, are all too familiar.

To dispel any myth regarding the success of the telephone we have only to recall the job-seekers sections of the newspapers and how over the past decade telesales vacancies have been increasingly advertised. It isn't just the smaller companies either. Large multinationals and corporations have enjoyed rapid expansion in the hands of this very tool. The importance of the telephone in serious business is well recognized, but many are still learning how best to use it for improving selling effectiveness.

How you view the telephone and the personnel using it is the very key to its success. We live in a world where records and achievements are constantly changing. What then are you afraid of? The flaw lies not so much with the phone but with its operator. To understand how the phone can work against you, try to examine your fears. Remember the quote, 'The thing to fear is fear itself'? Can you really afford to allow yourself that luxury? What is the very worst thing that can happen? You could receive a negative response – indeed someone may actually say 'No'. Of course nobody likes rejection, but think: is it you that is being rejected or is it your idea? You are representing your company in this contact. It is not a personal call, so you can't afford to take it personally.

Relax. Enjoy the game. The prospects/customers are more disadvantaged. They have to make serious buying decisions based on the information they gain. To keep abreast of their own competitive marketplace they have to be aware of options open to them and are therefore more kindly disposed to listen. If, however, they decide to use another provider on this occasion you haven't lost. Simply keep the door open by suggesting a future call (on an agreed date) when a review would be appropriate and buying decisions could be reassessed. Few people will refuse – they can't afford to.

2

THE ATTITUDE (YOURS!)

Getting into the right frame of mind is not as easy as it sounds. Some people seem to be, and are, naturally self-motivated. Highly motivated individuals often have clear personal goals, which they seek to achieve through their performance. You only have to look at entrepreneurs such as Bill Gates. The key to motivation, quite simply, is inspiration. Yes, our work provides us with a means to an end and many work to live, but there is more to motivation than monetary reward. Our work takes up a great deal of our waking life.

People with ill-defined goals are less able to identify with their work and this obviously reduces effort. Take time to analyse the purpose of one of your calls. What do you hope to achieve? By having specific aims, you as an individual are more able to measure your performance. Recognizing well-defined goals increases self-motivation, which in turn develops enthusiasm. The single most important aspect in good communication is enthusiasm, which comes from the Greek words *'en theo'* meaning 'inner god'. In other words, the capacity to succeed comes from within. If it is applied correctly it breeds confidence, which in turn instils a powerful motivating force in the people we communicate with, ie it encourages positive feedback from our prospects.

SWOT analysis

Whenever you need to assess a concept or situation, a good tool to use is a SWOT analysis. In any exercise connected with improvement you have to find ways to maximize *strengths*, minimize *weaknesses*, explore and seize *opportunities* and plan strategies to overcome/avoid *threats*. Your SWOT analysis will provide you with this information. Simply create four headings:

'S' – strengths;

'W' – weaknesses;

'O' – opportunities;

'T' – threats.

Think about what you want to achieve from using the telephone, and make lists under these headings. This will help you analyse the areas you need to concentrate on to improve your performance.

Consider also perceptions. First, look at your customers and what they represent (there's more on this in the next chapter) and secondly, look at the service/product you provide as a company, department and possibly as an individual member of the team.

The more information you acquire the clearer you will become about how motivated and confident you are. Think about it: the more confident you are, the more you strive to achieve; the more successful you become, the more enthusiastic and aware you are; and the more practised you are, the further you develop your proficiency. It's a cycle and it all leads to building confidence. Without self-confidence you will be unable to instil enthusiasm and confidence in the prospect.

However, do remember that no matter how expert you become there are a few pitfalls to be aware of. For example, customers are only interested in their own problems. You also need to avoid competing with them in the knowledge test. No matter how sure you are of your facts, 'one-upmanship' is a dangerous tool.

Similarly, don't allow your enthusiasm to lead to familiarity. Developing rapport is important, but if, for example, you discover you have a common interest such as a sport, don't be tempted to share too much of your knowledge – the call is not a personal one. The balance between being professional and not is a fine one. Better to acknowledge common ground, allow the client some floor space and then move on to or back to the business agenda.

The effects of attitude

Your attitude affects not only your own feelings but also those of your customers. It also affects the attitude of your colleagues. How you conduct yourself will have a 'knock-on' effect on those you are in contact with both verbally and visually – just as the attitude of the company will affect how the organization is perceived.

Most companies see themselves in the classic pyramid structure. Customers provide the base of the pyramid, then come the contacts (sales/marketing/support), next the supervisors and managers, and finally on to directors and the MD. In fact in a customer-driven organization this should be reversed. Company members should help colleagues on to the next tier to do a better job. If you are the MD you should be guiding, helping and demonstrating how important customers are and how important the telephone is as a tool in gaining a greater understanding of them. We all need to get to know our customers better. We need to be more objective than subjective – in other words, to communicate more openly.

Your attitude to your customers and the phone as a tool to create and sustain business will filter through the company and indeed to your prospects. People sense if you are not committed to a customer. The attitude *must* be genuine. It is too easy to 'run customers down' when you've received a few difficult calls. To encourage the right attitude in yourself you need to start making necessary changes. Are you committed to change? We live in a world of constant change. The business environments in which we work are becoming increasingly competitive. Our position in the market and indeed our market share will undoubtedly have changed since the business began. We have to be flexible enough to adapt to those changes. Consider the following: 'A customer is the most important person in business' and, 'You are the most important person in the company' because you are in touch with the customer.

Motivation

With ever-increasing pressures to 'perform' and 'produce results' we can all too easily lose sight of the task in hand. The simplest route to success is through willingness and ability. If the desire doesn't come from within, your response to change will only be short term. People revert back to their old ways and what they want to do long term. You have to want to change. Many of the techniques used here, once adapted and applied, are used in sales and indeed any form of direct people communication. Apply them then not only to yourself but to your customer too.

How? By raising your level of aspiration you create the will 'to do', which means that you will be internally motivated to meet the requirements of success. But what is motivation? It quite simply refers to the constructive effort by which we incite, from within, a positive and successful action. The four basic motivating forces are as follows:

- the need to be appreciated;
- the fear of disapproval or rejection;
- the mechanism of curiosity;
- the need to identify.

Ability

Performance equals ability and incentive. In other words, what people do (their performance) is the product of what they can do (ability) and what they will do (incentive).

So, we have looked at attitude and motivation, but what of ability? Ability consists of two things: 1) knowledge, 2) skill in using that knowledge. To improve our ability in tele-sales we need to examine these two areas.

Knowledge

There are four types of knowledge that sales people must possess:

- product knowledge – what they are selling;
- knowledge of their market – who they are selling to;
- knowledge of the competition – who else is selling a similar product;
- knowledge of the principles and techniques of successful selling.

Skills

These can be broken into three key areas:

- selling skills – being practised in the principles and techniques of selling;
- judgement skills – sizing up people and situations; distinguishing between what people say and what they mean;
- human relationship skills – the ability to get along with others.

These must be developed individually and independently through experience and practice.

Learning new skills

But how do we learn? And indeed how do we enlighten (teach) our prospects about the merits of conducting business with us?

A great phenomenon of life is that from the moment we are born through to our last breath we are always learning. We start by grasping fundamentals – motor skills, language, etc. Then we receive education – facts and information walking hand in hand with our own experiences in life and our parental direction. Finally we mature and recognize that expertise and 'know how' is ongoing.

Psychologists say there are four main areas through which we acquire our knowledge:

- our own experiences;
- observations;
- concepts and generalizations;
- activity.

To lead by example (ie to encourage our prospects and to motivate them) we have to have the right attitude. This attitude triggers our awareness so that we can develop these four areas in the individual.

3

THE CUSTOMER

Having just considered the psychology behind motivation and learning in our work, we now need to apply the technique to our customers. It is necessary that we give information in the appropriate way to allow and help customers to make valued decisions.

To do this we need to understand what motivates customers to absorb information in a particular way. Strictly speaking we want to get them to learn about us in a positive way. Learning, however, is a voluntary action, so how do you get people to start, to continue and to come back tomorrow? The same disciplines can be applied to the seller and buyer alike – look at the parallels:

Telesales people	Customers
People don't just work for money	Customers don't just buy something because it's cost effective

Telesales people want reward – a sense of achievement, mastery of their work, status to give them an incentive

Customers want to think they've made a good buying decision

What keeps them at it? That encouraging feeling that they're achieving or getting the hang of it

Once a customer has bought, a relationship can be developed. New products can be offered, or the service provided can be developed in the knowledge that their decisions are good ones

Once they've felt achievement today they will want to come back tomorrow for the same buzz

The satisfaction a customer gains will motivate loyalty and a continued working relationship

Understanding your customers

The core to providing customers with a good service is to provide harmony. Harmony turns customers who are 'satisfied' into ones who are 'delighted'. Relate to your customers. They are human beings too. They suffer from the same anxieties, hopes, fears and aspirations as you. All too easily we prejudge. Make sure you show empathy – relate to your customers. Put yourself in their shoes. Ask yourself what you'd be looking for in their situation – your answer will usually give you the solution you seek. Customers – and suppliers, who are our customers too – are vital to our business success.

So who are our customers? They, quite literally, are people who come back a second time and more to do business with us. You're probably thinking that this seems so obvious; if so, you are likely to be someone who is competent, motivated and able.

Consider the following steps in the learning process:

1. Unconscious Incompetence.

2. Conscious Incompetence.

3. Conscious Competence.

4. Unconscious Competence.

Remember learning a new skill – driving a car for example. You start not knowing what is expected of you. You've never sat in the driver's seat, had any lessons or indeed shown any great interest before. Now you've decided to learn, but you are 'unconsciously incompetent' (number 1 in the list above) – you don't yet know what's involved and are not yet able.

After your first lesson, you realize that to drive is an acquired skill. A great deal of concentration is required and you'll have to practise hand–eye co-ordination to use the mirrors, gears, indicators, etc properly. Not only that, you have to consider weather conditions, pedestrians, other vehicles, the type of road/area and so on. You are now conscious of what is expected but probably (after one lesson anyway) not yet able, so you are now 'consciously incompetent' (number 2).

The next step – you've reached the driving test stage. You've had a number of lessons and feel ready to be examined. Hopefully you pass first time. Do you remember that test? Most of us do. We are so in tune with what is required. Everything is fresh in our minds and we drive along listening to the examiner's instructions and acting accordingly. We know what is required and how to handle it. We are 'consciously competent' (number 3).

Finally, having passed – hooray! – we are able to drive unsupervised. We become more confident each day and eventually we drive automatically. How many of us drive a familiar route each day, say from home to work, and remember or register how many sets of traffic lights we passed, how many we had to stop at, how many round-abouts, red cars, or dogs on leads we saw? Need I go on? We've become 'unconsciously competent' (number 4) but we've also become dangerous drivers! Be honest – how many of us are confident we'd pass if we had to repeat our driving test tomorrow?

So what's happened? We're experienced. We're able. What's the problem? Dare I say we've become complacent. So much in our lives becomes so familiar that we sit back and relax. That's fine except when we relax too much we lose sight of things. Our customers are equally guilty. Buying decisions may already form a regular pattern or routine. They probably haven't had the time to analyse this for a while. Resourcing and updating should become a regular and integral part of one's work.

So, just as we need to have objectives in mind when we speak to customers, we need to consider what's going through their mind. What sort of thoughts are they likely to have? Make a list, for example, 'I don't know enough about the company/staff/service/reputation, etc to make a valued judgement'.

Customers are people like you or me. To try to understand them better, what they are like, how they perceive us and so on, it would help to examine ourselves. Our own inner self gives us all the clues we need to demonstrate empathy. You have to get close to your customer at a very early stage to stand a better chance of making a sale and equally importantly, forming a long-term relationship.

Identifying customer needs

Many telesales people avoid asking customers what they want because they're frightened they won't be able to provide it. Yet if you meet the needs of your customers they will be satisfied, are likely to return to you and, just as importantly, they will communicate about you favourably to colleagues and other businesses – all of whom are your potential clients. Word of mouth is a very powerful marketing tool and it costs nothing!

So what are customers generally looking for?

Reliability

They want to be sure you can be relied upon to do whatever it is they are requesting and within the appropriate timescale. They also want to be certain that the advice you give is correct.

Credibility

Show customers that they are not guinea pigs by demonstrating how much you do for other companies and people like them. Also mention any relevant accreditation/awards you have achieved that show a real measure of your worth.

Professionalism

Are behaviour, advice, customer handling, delivery, etc carried through in an acceptably proficient way? The real professional demonstrates this by illustrating the whole picture.

Efficiency

The speed at which you take orders, refer on, sort problems, carry out instructions and so on shows you do not waste the customers' valuable time. Efficiency plays an important part in projecting the right image.

Value for money

Let's face it, we're all looking for this, whether we are rummaging through jumble at a church sale or buying a new car. Value for money is also reflected in time and how it is used. Time, especially in business, costs. If you are efficient with time it will be recognized. Your time is also valuable. How well you use it will often reflect in results, so money is another measure here.

Be positive

Being positive will be important to your conversation. When two people are talking, possibly for the first time, one usually takes the initiative. In sales it has to be you. Positivity reflects professionalism, confidence and enthusiasm. These qualities encourage the recipient (customer) to listen. You'll be in control. People who are positive and combine this with charm, encounter fewer difficulties because the advice of a professional is usually relied upon. Think of your GP – you don't know him (or her) but you give him information about yourself while he listens and makes notes. He then tells you what's wrong, offers a remedy and you go away happily trusting the advice. The relationship you want to develop with your customer is similar. You too will need to guide your customer down a certain route.

The target

Next, start reviewing your objectives. Think about what you want to achieve from the call:

- Do you want to get orders? If so, how many? By when? From whom?

- Do you want to arrange a sales appointment? If so, with whom? By when? And where?

- Do you want to get information? If so, what sort? How and from whom?

- How is your customer likely to respond?

Ask yourself whether you will achieve your objectives in your first approach or if you are likely to need to contact the customer several times, using just the phone or a combination of approaches. Keep your target in mind. You can't *make* (potential) customers buy, visit, impart information, or accept an appointment, but you can guide them to want to do so. You can create a desire in them to take the necessary action to proceed.

4

THE APPROACH

A thought to ponder:

We speak at around 120 words/minute.

We read at around 200 words/minute.

We listen at around 400 words/minute.

Don't waste the differential. The listener's mind is only partially engaged. In fact, when we speak to someone over the telephone, we use only 25 per cent of their listening capacity, for a variety of reasons:

- We are dealing with a piece of apparatus that's transmitting our voice. Part of the clarity of the voice is lost in the transmission.

- People have the capacity to listen to several things at once, including being aware of other conversations and outside sounds such as traffic.

- Concentration spans vary and people can allow their minds to wander and fill with their own thoughts.

- Distractions can impede people's listening as their focus wanders.

Influencing powers

Do you know why people do business with your firm? It helps if you can establish how they became influenced. Usually, if you can put customers' minds at rest when you first speak to them you have a much better chance of success. Consider then where influence is most powerful:

- 7% of our influence comes through the words we use;

- 38% of our influence comes through our voice qualities;

- 55% of our influence comes through the use of body language.

Because we lose the most influential factor – body language – over the phone, the ratio shifts as follows: 25 per cent through vocabulary and 75 per cent through voice qualities (how we sound).

Customers' tolerance levels are much lower over the phone than they are face-to-face. As they cannot see us, they have to rely on mental pictures that we create for them, using our voice and vocabulary. It's quite a tall order. As far as customers are concerned, if we can't give them what they want, they will go elsewhere.

The customer wants to make a decision that is easy to make – whether it's to purchase something or seek information. Consider the psychology. Is your approach making the customer feel that the glass is 'half full' or that it's 'half empty'?

Vocabulary

The vocabulary we use is so important. We all use negative words and phrases like 'I think', 'maybe', 'could', etc. In isolation they can be very dangerous. Imagine if, having been asked your opinion, you tell a customer that 'It may work for you'.

Occasionally you have to use negative words. If delivery is scheduled for Thursday but the client would prefer to receive the order by Wednesday afternoon, you can't guarantee it, but you can use positive phraseology to help – 'I'll try to get this to you by Wednesday by putting in a special request with the driver. If he can accommodate he will. If not it will definitely be with you on Thursday.' You could even add (if appropriate and accurate): 'Most of our special requests are met, so it's likely that you will have it on Wednesday.' You haven't committed yourself but the customer sees that every effort is being made to be accommodating. How you are perceived is everything.

Positive means 'actioning' or 'doing', for example, 'The best idea for you…', 'What we can do…', 'What you need …', 'Others have found…'. What you say and how you say it is very influential. Consider a barrister in court. He or she uses language to the extreme. The prosecution leads the witness in such a way that you believe the accused guilty, then the defence counsel, with the same information, takes over and leads the witness in an equally convincing way and you now believe the accused is innocent.

You will need to advise and guide your clients without actually making decisions for them. So next time, before you speak, *stop* and think about what you are about to say. Customers want to feel comfortable and those of us who can communicate to good effect will enjoy the competitive edge.

Mirroring

Listen to the way your voice changes in different situations and monitor the reactions it gains. The way you sound influences the way you are received. Consider a mother talking to a child and saying, 'Yes, I'm very pleased with you.' Depending on the intonation and emphasis on the word 'very', she can leave the child in no doubt that she is far from pleased. Tune into your customer's voice.

By far the most powerful way to make a good impression is to create rapport, which can only exist when two or more people show harmony – a mutual feeling of well-being and understanding. Next time you sit in a restaurant, watch couples (discretely!) and you'll soon recognize the ones who are getting along well. Notice how they make eye contact, angle their heads in the same way, lift a glass together, and when one begins to eat the other does as well and with the same sort of movement. They are mirroring each other. But it isn't just their body language. They speak in the same tone, pace the conversation in the same way, use the same vocabulary and phraseology, even pause in the same rhythm – their pacing demonstrates rapport.

To make mirroring or rapport work over the phone you must create an open and honest conversation, listening carefully to the voice, sound and content of the prospects' answers and questions. Meet them on their own level to make them feel at ease. Think about the skills and techniques you must develop so that you can achieve this without sounding insincere or patronizing. A pattern will begin to emerge. Like-minded people mix together. Rapport is based on mutual respect. You both need to relate to each other, yet you are the one who is going to have to engineer the process. Remain positive. It will emerge fairly quickly what the differences and similarities are between you. If you become negative you will merely highlight those differences in the customer's mind. By remaining positive you are concentrating on the similarities between you. Concentrating your efforts in this way will develop that understanding which helps people bond.

We cannot, however, agree with everything or we lose credibility, but we do want to show we understand. The best tool to establish this is by mirroring or duplicating actions or statements. It shows that we see and share the other person's very real hopes, fears, worries, expectations, etc. To be agreeable is not condescending but shows true empathy – meeting people on their own ground so that they feel in unison with us. By mastering the technique you'll find that you can engage your customer in a favourable way.

The two key areas in mirroring over the phone are: 1) *voice mirroring* through pitch, volume, tone, pacing, vocabulary, phraseology, tempo, etc; and 2) *emotional mirroring* through attitude, belief, tolerance, understanding, compatibility through respect, involvement, sharing qualities, etc. Your personality and the way you relate to the customer can help influence the impression you give. For example, if you are in an organization that provides a product or service that is identical to that supplied by another firm, why would a prospect buy from you as opposed to the direct competition? The answer, quite simply, is because of you. *You* are the company, product, service. How you relate to the customer will largely determine the results of the call. In conclusion then – how you view the customer will reflect how you yourself are viewed.

Difficulties

Occasionally there will be clashes. In any difficult situation there is always a danger that the stress it causes and the way that makes us feel as individuals will mean that we take the call personally. While we want to show rapport, we must remember that this is a business-to-business arrangement. Show empathy (by putting yourself into the customer's shoes) but remember this is not a social call or family event and we cannot afford the luxury of allowing ourselves to take it personally. If we do, we lose control.

As no two customers will be the same, you will not be able to achieve uniformity in your approach, but you can develop a style and remain consistent. Remember the idea of a game – knowing the rules, then developing and building on them. There are two areas to help you do this while keeping the company's reputation intact. First, *enthusiasm* – this is the single most powerful influencing tool. Anyone who speaks with enthusiasm, knowingly or not, opens windows of opportunity. It rubs off. If you're enthusiastic it's difficult to create a negative response. Secondly, *confidence* – the more positive the feedback, the more confident you will be. Like enthusiasm, it rubs off. Customers want to be involved with a company they feel safe with and they can trust.

Preparation

By now you should be in the right frame of mind to start thinking about the actual call. Remember – if a job is worth doing, it's worth doing well.

We talked about leading the customer and a number of ways we could help ourselves to do this: getting into the right emotional/mental attitude; thinking like the customer;

empathy and rapport; confidence and enthusiasm. These are all subjective, intangible, but very positive aspects of our preparation. They deal with emotion. We can also prepare more tangible aspects of the call. Here are some practical areas to help the conversation.

Product/prices/competitors

Know your product (or service) and prices, and those of your competitors. Knowing your rivals in the market helps keep you one step ahead. If your prospect is unsure who to buy from, you will have the advantage because you will understand why he or she is having difficulties reaching a decision. With this knowledge you can highlight the benefits of your company to help sway the results in your favour. Belief in your product/service is equally important – if you are convinced, you are more likely to convince your client.

Testimonials

Keep records of other clients who have used you successfully and keep updating the information when you talk to your regular customers. This is solid evidence. By relaying factual information to potential clients about the successes of your other clients, who may well be their competitors, they are more likely to buy – you will have removed any doubts and increased your credibility.

Questions

If the information prospects give is vague, ask searching questions to find out more. The questions should be open-ended and start with 'Why?', 'How?', 'When?', 'Where?', 'Who?'. You are unlikely to succeed in selling if you have limited information. Prepare questions that will give you the information you need.

Objections

Anticipate reasons why prospects may decide not to buy from you. List difficulties experienced in the past and examine ways in which you best handled them. Pre-empting objections will help you be more fluent in your response.

Information pointer/word tracks

Points of reference are useful to help prompt you in the call. The prospect can't see you, so you can make notes before and during the call that will prompt you and enable you to recap. Information pointers should contain guideline questions, presentation points, selling phrases and closes. They should follow the pattern of the sale examined in the next chapter. You can adapt and change the information as you discover ways to improve it.

Warning: you must not write lengthy sentences and read them out verbatim – it will make you sound like a parrot and you'll not only lose credibility but will find it a less comfortable and less spontaneous conversation.

Remember: 'Nobody plans to fail, they just fail to plan.'

5

THE SALE

All customers are important. There are two main marketing tasks in any business – attracting new customers and retaining existing ones. At least five times more time and money is spent on a new prospect/customer than a current/existing one. Both are essential. Getting the balance right and retaining customers makes good economic sense.

The telephone is quite versatile and can be used in a variety of ways. You may need to make appointments over the phone – sometimes face-to-face presentations are more appropriate and you can use the phone to set that up. The procedure is called 'telemarketing'. The phone can also be used to procure business; it's often 'cold calling' (ringing out for the first time) and it creates the most difficulties. One way you can overcome the hurdle is to practise on existing clients by servicing the account – making sure you phone them regularly rather than relying on them phoning you when they require something. Another way is by 'selling up' and 'adding to' their existing orders. In other words, check that you have maximized on the call.

Incoming calls

One of the main advantages of customers phoning in is that they are doing so in a buying frame of mind. They may merely be enquiring about prices, but you have the opportunity to speak to them. Your task is to maintain the conversation – without it there is a real danger that no sale will be made as communication dwindles. Use phrases to recap or maintain attention, such as:

'I appreciate how you feel.'

'You have a point, of course.'

'If I understand you correctly...'

'So what you are saying is...'

'Based on what you have said you need...'

By being positive and leading the caller you will find that you will also be able to end the call more professionally. When you pick up the phone begin with an enthusiastic and cheerful greeting, for instance: 'Good morning, The Garden Company, may I help you?' This also allows the caller to acknowledge they have the right number.

Prospect: 'I want some information about garden sheds.'

Telesales person: 'You're through to the right person, my name is Alex and you are?'

Prospect: 'Mr Vetch.'

Telesales person: 'How may I help you, Mr Vetch?'

Prospect: 'I want the price of your garden sheds.'

At this stage the telesales person has the prospect's name and is using it to break the formality. She does not yet know whether the prospect is phoning other centres and comparing prices. Assuming this garden centre stocks a large range of garden sheds, questions need to be asked to ascertain what type of shed is required and what type of shed will suit the prospect. Although people will buy what they perceive to be beneficial to them (something that satisfies the 'What's in it for me?' syndrome), don't lose credibility by selling the top end of the range if a less expensive shed will serve the purpose. Look after the prospect's purse strings and they will relate better to you.

> *Telesales person:*   'What do you intend using it for,
> Mr Vetch?'

This open question helps to establish whether the shed is for commercial or private use and whether a larger, stronger or smaller shed would be suitable. By adding the prospect's name at the end of the question you include a personal touch.

Occasionally the prospect may resent questions – he or she may have a preconceived idea of what is needed and through impatience appears gruff. Do not become disconcerted. Explain that you are asking these questions to find out which type of shed would best suit the needs of the prospect, who obviously doesn't want anything that is unsuitable.

You cannot talk about the benefits of your product/service until you have established the need. You do this through selective questioning:

> 'Which part of your house faces north?'

> 'How often do you cater for large numbers?'

> 'When is your financial year-end?'

Once you have established relevant information you will need to clarify the situation by restating your findings (the needs of the prospect) so that it is reinforced in their mind: 'So you review your employee benefits at the beginning of the new financial year, is that right?' The clarification is ended with a question so that the client can confirm with a 'Yes'. If the answer is 'No', then you can ask more questions to find the right need.

If the answer is 'Yes', then you have arrived at the selling stage and now have the opportunity to tell the prospect what's available. Avoid phrases like 'I advise' or 'I recommend' as your personal feelings are irrelevant and there is a real danger this could backfire on you if subsequently the product doesn't fulfil the requirements – you will be blamed. Better to demonstrate the merits and suitability by giving examples of customers or other situations where this has been successfully applied. Your presentation of the product/service should be filled with relevant facts and carefully selected benefits to remain totally professional. Enthusiasm is infectious, so ensure you know your product inside out and use your information pointer.

If you do not complete the sale at this enquiry stage, don't worry. By extending your advice but leaving the door open the prospect may well come back. Better still, arrange to phone them back after an agreed time lapse to review/discuss further.

Cold calls

Regular clients and incoming calls generate 'bread and butter' income. In order to maintain and even expand your market share you need to contact new prospects. This is called 'cold calling'.

Once you've decided who to call it is important that you speak to the decision maker. If you don't already know who that is, simply call the firm and ask: 'Hello, would you tell me who (the personnel manager) is?' Or: 'Who is responsible for (buying/organizing stationery)?'

Once you have the name, write it down so that you can use it when you speak:

Telesales person: 'I see, would you put me through to Mr Simpson please?'

Secretaries – friend or foe?

Sometimes you are put through, but often calls are screened. Don't try selling to anyone other than the decision maker. By the time the message has been relayed it is second-hand and won't be delivered with the same conviction or with the correct technique. It is important, however, to keep on the right side of secretaries/receptionists. They have the power to put you through. They also know that they are not the decision maker, and you can turn that to your advantage:

Secretary: 'Hello, Mr Evans' secretary.'
Telesales person: 'Hello, this is Jane Hughes from Jacksons, may I speak to Mr Evans please?'
Secretary: 'What's it in connection with?'
Telesales person: 'Well, we manufacture metal sheeting, as you probably know, and I understand that Mr Evans is in charge of the supplies. Is he there?'

So, nothing is hidden. You have shown sensitivity to her role but also illustrated and confirmed together that indeed Mr Evans is the person to speak to (if not, she will tell you who is).

Secretary: 'Well, he's in a meeting right now.'
Telesales person: 'When would be a good time to call back?'
Secretary: 'After 2 pm.'
Telesales person: 'I'll call back after 2 pm then. Thank you for your help.'

You will have remained in control and not allowed any uncomfortable pauses. You have also arranged a convenient call-back time when the secretary will be obliged to put you through – provided you keep the appointment!

Other secretaries may ask, 'Can I help?' Again, keep the call harmonious and say, 'Yes you can.' This confirms that you respect their position. 'My director has asked me to contact your boss. Perhaps you can tell me when he will be free and I'll call back?' This will either prompt a time or the 'Can I help?' example just covered. The rapport with the secretary will have a significant impact on your success rate in getting through. If you are rejected outright, don't be disconcerted. Practice helps!

AIDA

You are now ready to achieve your objective. You either want the customer to buy, or arrange a visit, or impart information, or complete a questionnaire, but you can't force them. You can't make them do it but you can make them *want* to do it. That is, you can create the desire in them to act (take the decision). Before you can do this you must generate enough interest in them to create that desire. That is, interest leads to desire, which leads to action. But in the first instance, as you have not been invited to call them and they are not expecting to hear from you, you must initially grab their attention. This is a well-established and successful method of selling known as AIDA – quite simply it means you grab the prospect's *attention* by stimulating *interest* in your product/service, and then by identifying benefits, the prospect *desires* the offer and takes the necessary *action* to purchase.

Many firms send out mailshots to precede calls. This is largely a personal choice, although certain products need to be seen before they are purchased. Whatever the initial decision, the call itself should follow the same AIDA pattern.

Attention

Introduce yourself and clarify the prospects' position.

'I am Laraine from JJD and understand you handle the marketing for the firm. Is that right?' First impressions count. The strength of the opening is vital. A call from you is not expected. The prospect is busy and merely saying, 'I'd like to talk to you about our new lines' is not going to establish two-way communication.

When you watch a film or go to a concert you know within the first few minutes whether it's going to be compelling. The same applies in sales. The customer listens more to the first question than any other. A security systems firm that opens its approach with 'Would you be interested in buying a burglar alarm?' is less likely to get a positive response. A better angle would be: 'Burglary has increased by 10 per cent over the last 12 months. When was the last time you heard of a local robbery?' Equally, a corporate pensions adviser asking 'Are you happy with your current provision?' will not succeed. A negative response is being prompted. Better to say, 'How often do you review your pension provision?' The inference here is that review is something that surely does take place. To deny review is to deny progress. In each example the second question will be more successful because neither is a closed question inviting 'Yes/No' responses. They are both open questions. Openness increases awareness and can be offered in a variety of ways. There are several methods of questioning:

- Open questions – used to open out conversations and gather information. They prompt a full response by not allowing one-word reactions. They usually start with the question words 'Who?', 'Why?', 'Where?', 'When?', 'How?'

- Closed questions – are more useful for establishing a specific point and can help create rapport, close a conversation or get a commitment or decision. 'Have you received our catalogue?' would then be followed by an open question.

- Probing or 'building' questions – gather more information by getting a customer to develop a previous answer. Examples might include, 'Could you tell me about…?', 'Will you elaborate on that for me?', or 'In your opinion tell me…'.

- Linking questions – require active listening. They are the kind of question that can change the direction of the conversation and introduce a new subject by linking back to earlier responses: 'You mentioned earlier…', 'Tell me…'. Other useful techniques include reflecting – especially useful when emotions are running high. You simply reflect the customers' feeling back to them: 'I'm sure you were happy about that.' It's also useful for recapping: 'So what you're saying is…'.

Interest

Once you've aroused attention you need to establish interest so that you can discover the likely need the prospect has of your product/service. Effective questioning is the key to establishing and maintaining good two-way communication. Correct use of the various types is critical. Keep the conversation positive. Look at the following and think of examples that relate to you:

Closed (negative)		_Open_ (positive)
'Do you want red?'	becomes	'Which colour would you prefer?'
'Shall we visit in the morning?'	becomes	'When is the best time to visit?'

'Do you have an account?'	becomes	'What is your account number?'

Listening

Asking the right questions is vital but futile if you don't *listen* to the answers. Unless someone listens to the message and understands it, there is no communication, only noise. Also, if you are too anxious to put your point across you may miss vital clues. Listening, or non-verbal communication, complements questioning and it acknowledges and shows approval of what the other person is saying.

Take notes and respond with either further appropriate questions to gather more information or suggest ways in which the prospect can be helped by buying your product. The number of questions varies. The important point is that you ask enough to illustrate the prospect's need. Once you've done this it's important to get him or her to agree to this.

You can also use 'tie-downs' to commit the prospect. These are useful selling phrases such as 'Isn't it?', 'Doesn't it?', 'Won't it?', 'Can't you?' and so on. Once the customer has agreed, it's very difficult for him or her to say 'No'. If the customer does object at some later stage, you will have something to draw him or her back to: 'As you've already agreed Mr (or Mrs) Smith, you would welcome extra business, wouldn't you?' or 'You mentioned earlier that you need an idea to help unburden you of your paperwork, isn't that right?'

A telesales person selling personalized Christmas cards could tackle it like this:

Telesales person: 'Would it be true to say that your company has expanded to a national market because of the quality products you offer?'

49

Prospect: 'Yes – and competitive prices. Word travels fast.'

Telesales person: 'You obviously have a good image then.' (Pause.) 'What about goodwill?'

Prospect: 'Oh yes, our customers know we care for them.'

Telesales person: 'At Christmas, Mr Jones, would you say goodwill was more important or less?'(You've loaded the question to provoke the response 'more' – no one is going to say 'less'.)

Prospect: 'More. We offer special Christmas discounts to our customers.'

Telesales person: 'That's a good idea for those customers who are prepared to buy at that time. What about your clients who don't buy in the winter?'

Prospect: 'Um, well the offer's there.' (Now he's unsure – the telesales person must establish that need verbally.)

Telesales person: 'To maintain your image, especially during Christmas, you could do with something that extends your goodwill to all your customers, couldn't you?' (The tie-down demands a positive answer leaving the path clear to proceed.)

Prospect: 'Yes, I suppose so.'

Telesales person: 'That's exactly why I'm ringing.'

The number of questions you ask during the interest stage will vary from call to call. With practice you will be more flexible and able to adapt this vital stage. Once you have the necessary information you can move on.

Desire

If you use an approach like the example above, the customer will listen because you have committed him o her. The information pointer can be more detailed here – learn it, so that your own personality is exposed, don't read it. You are now in a position to give a presentation, but remember that people will buy the same things but for different reasons. Choose the right benefits and don't disguise them – people will buy a specific benefit (ie what something offers them) to satisfy a specific need. In this part of the sale there are *selling points* and *benefits.*

A selling point is a manufactured quality or what it actually is. A benefit is what it will do for you. For example, a chair may be cushioned – that's a fact that won't change. The benefit could be that it's comfortable. People buy benefits and we link the two phrases using the words 'which means'. You are selling in three key areas: the company; the product; the staff. List your own benefits under these headings.

Also at this stage think of a unique selling point or USP. This emphasizes a quality that is reputed to be unique to you. This may not be the case but because you have highlighted it, your prospect concludes that no one else offers this benefit; for example: 'We deliver free of charge on all orders over £XX', or 'We have a 24-hour help line.'

Testimonials

These are one of the best sales tools you can have as they offer firm evidence in support of your claim. Collect a list and regularly update it. Stories of other satisfied customers will help instil confidence in your prospect's mind. If you do not have a specific one, a more general one can be used, such as one promoting the image of the company.

Buying signals

A buying signal is an indication by a customer that they are keen to go ahead with the purchase or are at least interested. They may use verbal nods of approval like 'Oh', or actual commitments such as, 'That sounds good', or it may be disguised in a question: 'What about delivery?' or 'I've heard you only sell by the roll.' They can come at any stage in the sale and once you've spotted them, act on them.

Cost

If you have not already been asked about cost by the time you present benefits, proceed naturally to the price. Never be afraid of telling the customer how much. If you are wary of it, your customers will detect this in your tone of voice and it will cast doubts in their mind; your hesitation will be received negatively. People value something by the value that is put on it. Emphasize the value the customer is gaining by either sandwiching the price, 'On an order of 10 you pay only £XX, making an additional saving of £X', or by breaking the cost down into palatable measures, 'As the guarantee is for 10 years, it works out at less than £XX per week.'

Action

Once the cost has been presented, tie up the order. Nothing is sold until you get that final commitment. Asking, 'Do you want me to send them to you?' or, 'Shall I go ahead and book that for you?' is inviting a negative response. There are various types of closes you can use to secure the order.

Assumptive

This should be a continuation of the guidance you have offered throughout the sale: 'I'll have that sent to you next Thursday' or, 'Who shall I send the invoice to?'

Alternative

As the name implies, you give the customer an alternative. Whichever one he or she chooses, he or she has bought. 'Would you prefer delivery on Tuesday or Thursday?' The customer has to make a positive decision. Once you've asked the question, remain silent. The customer is then forced to agree. If not, you will have an objection to deal with, which we'll examine later.

Closing the sale becomes instinctive and can occur at any time in the sale. Provided the AIDA sequence is adhered to the results should be positive.

Telemarketing

Another area in which the telephone business function has evolved is that of telemarketing. Instead of selling the product or service over the phone (you omit the desire stage), an appointment is made for either yourself or a colleague to visit and talk in more detail. In recent years the potential of telemarketing has been recognized by professionals as diverse as chemists, surveyors, solicitors and engineers, as a way of developing networks in their field. Many of these professionals tackle the procedure themselves and in so doing illustrate that to sell requires special qualities, not qualifications.

Once again the key is the right attitude. You don't need technical experts to make the appointments, just good communicators. In fact, lack of knowledge can be an advantage – it will support your claim that the prospect needs to see an expert. The AIDA techniques are once again applied, but this time you're selling the idea of the prospect spending a little time with you or a representative, by arranging a visit. Your prospect's time is valuable – time is money. The close is the booking of the appointment.

Successful communicators don't waffle; rather they talk in short sentences and even in highlighted points. The prospects you contact are in a position of authority. To make

53

important buying decisions they need to keep abreast of the competition and are therefore more open to discussion. Give them a reason to make the appointment, ie what they'll gain from the meeting. Be concise. As with the cold call, give a brief introduction. Ask open questions and inform the prospect about your company. Once you've established the need, conclude with 'We'd welcome the opportunity of visiting and discussing XY with you in more detail – when would be convenient?' or 'We'd like to be more specific so that when you next choose XY you'll be in an even better position to make an informed decision. When can we visit?'

Objections

Few customers buy without reservations. Generally objections occur because people are unsure that what you are offering is really going to satisfy their demand or fulfil their need. Very often this is because they have misunderstood you and are seeking more information. This can occur at any stage in the sale and the list of types is endless. Here are some examples:

'It's a quiet time of year.'

'I don't sell upmarket products.'

'I'm happy with my current provider.'

'It's too risky.'

'It's too expensive.'

'I'm not interested.'

You can write down the most common ones you experience and plan your answer. Often prospects will object simply because they are uncertain, and as a defence against 'being sold' anything, they throw in a 'red herring'. It is futile answering every objection raised because you end up sounding petty and argumentative. To concentrate on discovering what the real trouble is you need to ask: 'Apart from that you'd go ahead?' or 'If you had proof that this would (meet the need), you'd buy?' If the objection is less obvious – perhaps a regular customer has been decreasing their order – ask: 'Are you completely satisfied with us, Mr Yates?' or if you suspect a specific grievance: 'Are you happy with our delivery times, Mrs Jones?'

Once you have found the problem, you have a tangible objection on your hands, which is much easier to handle.

Another method showing you have empathy and are able to relate to a client/prospect is the 'feel/felt/found' technique. Quite simply you could say: 'I understand how you feel Mr Franks, other clients have felt (similarly), but in our experience we have found (this works).' This is an excellent technique and very easy to use. It qualifies the point, shows that the fear is not unusual but can be sorted out, and gives a measurable means to offering a solution.

Sample calls

In each example introduce yourself and your company – no one likes speaking to an unknown source – then proceed.

To a regular customer

Telesales person: 'Mrs Sharp, this is a courtesy call to check that everything is proceeding smoothly.'
Prospect: 'Thank you, yes.'
Telesales person: 'Last time we spoke we renewed your stationery contract. Since then we have opened a print service and it occurred to me that we could look after your personalized stationery now as well.'

Prospect: 'Well, we regularly use XY and we're very happy with them.'

Telesales person: 'I understand.' (Pause.) 'Mrs Sharp, you needn't change suppliers completely – just use us as a backup, then if the other firm ever encounters any difficulties, and as we keep regular stocks of your paper, we could step in. It would be so much more convenient.' (You're not actually forcing the issue but by outlining it in such a way it could prompt a rethink.)

Prospect: 'Well, we were about to order more comps slips. Would you be able to provide us with the completed order by the end of the week?'

Telesales person: 'Is that when you'd want it by?' (By turning the question back on the prospect like this you are forcing a decision. If you had merely answered 'Yes' to the question you would be allowing the prospect an exit to consider the proposal.)

Prospect: 'Yes.' (Sold!)

Telesales person: 'In that case we'll have it to you by Thursday for proofing and the finished assignment to you by Friday.'

To a prospect – making an appointment

Telesales person: 'Mr Richards, I understand you handle the computer training for your firm. Can you tell me, do you outsource occasionally?'

Prospect: 'Yes.' (If 'No' and you establish that they are happy with their own facilities, then to further the call would be pointless.)

Telesales person: 'Who are you using at the moment?' (You need to know who you are competing with – remember though, never to knock the competition.)

Prospect: 'JT Computing.'

Telesales person: 'How often do you review your arrangements?' (This is a loaded question and implies they surely do review – it is designed to prompt a less certain response.)

Prospect: 'We are very happy with the service we receive and aren't looking for alternatives.'

Telesales person: 'I'm not suggesting that you swap providers, but it's obviously important that you keep abreast of what's available in the marketplace. There may be occasions when you need support – perhaps a second provider to help in unforeseen circumstances.' (Or you could say, 'I imagine you have witnessed many changes since you have been in this role, and that you spent considerable time analysing before you finally decided on your current provider.' You are stating the obvious, but to reject something also takes due consideration.)

Prospect: 'Possibly.'

Telesales person: 'We specialize in helping companies like your own and would like to make an appointment with you to highlight what's available so that as and when the need arises you'd be able to get in touch with us.' (The prospect sees this as unthreatening and that it would be an advantage to learn more.) Then close and ask for the appointment:

Telesales person: 'When would be convenient for you, Mr Richards?'

Prospect: 'I'm free on Wednesday.'

Telesales person: 'Say 2 pm?'

Prospect: 'Fine.'

Cold calling – telesales

Telesales person: 'Mrs Clare, I understand you handle the staff recruitment for your firm. Is that correct?'

Prospect: 'Yes, but we don't use agencies.'

Telesales person: 'I understand a number of companies of your size have preferred to handle the whole recruitment procedure in-house in the past. However, we're finding more and more are so short of time that they are beginning to outsource the first steps of the procedure and then get involved at the shortlist stage – they can then make their own decisions. What percentage of time could be saved for you to do other equally important tasks if you could use this service?'

Prospect: 'I'm not sure.'

Telesales person: 'Let me put it another way. When you're recruiting, what percentage of applicants would you say are totally unsuitable for the job?'

Prospect: 'About 75 per cent.'

Telesales person: 'So that means that about three-quarters of the time spent on a recruitment drive is wasted.'

Prospect: 'I suppose it does.'

Telesales person: 'What type of vacancy do you have currently?'

Prospect: 'For a shop floor manager, but we have plans.'

Telesales person: 'We have been successfully dealing with companies like yours for many years now.' (This ignores the objection and also demonstrates they are not guinea pigs.) 'Not only have we built up a substantial candidate bank for various positions but we also link in with all the appropriate media. This means if a position needs to be advertised we can make the arrangements promptly. Also, once the ads are placed we have the manpower to collate the information and do the initial screening.'

Prospect: 'Yes, but this sounds expensive.'

Telesales person: 'I understand why you may think that, indeed a number of our customers ran an exercise to see how cost-effective our service is. We charge a fixed fee of £XY plus Z per cent of the successful candidate's first year's salary. On balance our customers found they saved over XX per cent on their own costs and the time saved released them to concentrate on other equally pressing issues.'

Prospect: 'Umm.' (A buying signal.)

Telesales person: 'You mentioned you have a position in mind for a shop floor manager.'

Prospect: 'Yes, our current manager is due to retire shortly.'

The telesales person then takes the details and closes the sale.

Word prompt/pointer/script

It is important to prepare guidelines in advance. Remember not to write full conversations; just fill in examples under the following headings that are tailored and relevant to you. Remember this must only be used as a guideline and you need to be completely flexible with it – just because you have several examples doesn't mean you must use them all!

Attention
Opening questions

*

*

*

Interest
Open questions to establish the need

*

*

*

Desire
Selling points and benefits

*

*

*

Action
Closes

*

*

*

Objections

*

*

*

6

THE FOLLOW-UP

How you regard yourself now is critical to the way in which your future calls will be received. You need to keep one step ahead. We live in a world where records and achievements are constantly improving. Selling by telephone is fast and you should aim for continuous improvement. Just as the brain controls the body, so too it controls the emotions. Being negative or pessimistic can promote fatigue, apathy and unhappiness. Optimism or being positive promotes a feeling of vitality, happiness and the ability to get out there and get cracking.

Here is a checklist of the key issues in successful telephone selling:

- Wipe the slate clean – be fresh for each new call.

- Don't take the call personally – this is a business arrangement.

- Empathize – relate to the customer.

- Put customers first – show them how much you value them.

- Show rapport – by mirroring, you reinforce client ease
- Have a plan – prepare the call; do your homework.
- Use AIDA – learn it, apply it and practise it.
- Evaluate – learn from your mistakes; monitor you progress.
- Leave the door open – create the opportunity to kee in touch with the prospect/client.
- Don't be afraid – it's a game; if you apply the rules it' a 'best seller'!
- And finally, remember –'If at first you don't succeed, tr try, and try again.'

Visit Kogan Page on-line

Comprehensive information on
Kogan Page titles

Features include

- complete catalogue listings,
  including book reviews and
  descriptions

- on-line discounts on a variety
  of titles

- special monthly promotions

- information and discounts on
  NEW titles and BESTSELLING titles

- a secure shopping basket facility
  for on-line ordering

- infoZones, with links and
  information on specific areas of
  interest

PLUS everything you need to know
about KOGAN PAGE

http://www.kogan-page.co.uk